Suicide Is Not An Option

Freedom Through Writing Poetry

Rodessa M. Baker

Printed in the US
Published by Harrod Publishing LLC

Suicide Is Not An Option – Freedom Through Writing Poetry

Rodessa M. Baker   ISBN 9798669076467

About The Author

Rodessa M. Baker was born on February 15, 1971, to Robert and Janis Baker (deceased). She is a native Washingtonian and resides in Washington. Rodessa has one sibling, Andrea L. Baker, and three beautiful children, Jairus D. Baker, Jeremiah M. Baker, and Ronesha D.A. Pugh. She attends Immanuel Church in Ministries, where Donna Fox Ridgley is the Pastor.

A very special thanks to my family and friends who support me. And to LaWanna Harrod, the publisher

‥ —————————————————————————. . . . .

What are suicidal feelings?

People feel suicidal for a variety of reasons, for example:

- Life has become too difficult or hopeless because of external events like a relationship break-up or the symptoms of a mental health problem.
- They are experiencing intrusive thoughts about suicide or hearing voices which instruct them to take their own life.

Used with permission - https://www.time-to-change.org.uk/about-mental-health/types-problems/suicidal-feelings

Help is available 1-800-273-8255- Speak with a counselor today

National Suicide Prevention Lifeline - Hours: Available 24 hours. Languages: English, Spanish.

My Personal Story

GIVE ME A MINUTE

What kind of mindset does someone have to be in to reach the point of suicide? After all, there may have been many people who have thought about suicide without ever attempting.

While it doesn't answer what drives someone to that ultimate decision, there is a concept called cognitive constriction that explains what happens in the brain during a suicidal crisis.

It's tough to fight with suicide because the brain is not letting you access your other ways of thinking, as if you're seeing through a straw, or wearing blinders. People in this state can't see beyond their circumstances and don't believe their pain will ever end. This is why we hear some suicide survivors say, "*I thought it was the only way out.*" This can be described as a mental toothache," because all you can think about is the pain you are experiencing in that tooth and convince that this pain will never end.

This mental distortion isn't permanent, but it often seems like that at the moment. That's part of the reason suicidal persons seek counsel to come up with safety plans to turn to in the time of crisis, which may consist of a list of people to contact and/or activities that will calm them down and provide a distraction.

Moving forward from depression means that I have to live my life consistently and bring closure to the things of my past. I've had to think differently about what my life could have, would have been. Sure, there were challenges, twists, turns, and I've had to duck more times than I want to remember. All I know is that God does have a plan for my life. Jeremiah 29:11-14 KJV

> *[11] For I know the thoughts that I think toward you, saith the LORD, thoughts of peace, and not of evil, to give you an expected end.*
>
> *[12] Then shall ye call upon me, and ye shall go and pray unto me, and I will hearken unto you.*
>
> *[13] And ye shall seek me, and find me, when ye shall search for me with all your heart.*
>
> *[14] And I will be found of you, saith the LORD: and I will turn away your captivity, and I will gather you from all the nations, and from all the places whither I have driven you, saith the LORD; and I will bring you again into the place whence I caused you to be carried away captive.*

With a Word spoken over my life, I didn't go through what I went through for it not to come to pass. I believe, no, I know, *"I am supposed to be here."*

Suicide carries isolation, hurt, and shame. It stings.

One of the gifts God has created from my experiences in dark places is the ability to pray for others in those same places, with credibility. I know what it feels like when giving up seems more accessible than facing another day. I know the numbness that replaces the desire to keep going. It's the moment your pain turns into desperation.

There is an incredible freedom and Love for *life* the Lord gives in place of fear and hopelessness. Yes, He has given it to me.

When He was on the cross, He felt the full weight of our struggles. He gets it. Hebrews 4:1,

> *Jesus has been tempted in every way, just as we are.*

Grace is the unmerited, undeserved favor of God.

He pursued me even in the darkest places and moments. He loved me too much to stop. I am *worth* the pursuit. If He had not pursued me, I would not be here today. God's not done with me. Instead of me trying to escape this world by leaving it, I've escaped this world by falling into the arms of a God who turned my pain into something greater.

Your life doesn't have to be something you run from. God will complete the beautiful story He has already started in you. We were created for more than barely making it through each day. We can have an abundant life through Jesus. John 10:10 says,

> *¹⁰ The thief cometh not, but for to steal, and to kill, and to destroy: I am come that they might have life, and that they might have it more abundantly.*

Satan, the enemy tried to sneak old lies into my head. Yep, I still have scars, hospital bills, and some scary memories. But I have something worth way more than any darkness could ever cover. I have the gift of a *story* that can help others who are in the same place I once was, and I have an appreciation for the life-saving grace of God. I have more grace than I know what to do with. These days, I tell you, I *love* my life, and I will keep living it. By His grace, I am *more* than a conqueror of anything this life can throw at me. Romans 8:37,

> *³⁷ Nay, in all these things we are more than conquerors through him that loved us.*

My friend, you are too! The best is yet to come,

Get this, God doesn't need what you've lost, because He has so much more for you. God is and will do new things in your life. We have compartmentalized so much in the corridors of our emotions, and then they surface. Yes, triggers do happen in unhealed areas of our lives because we didn't deal with it then. We must keep moving and pressing forward and keep going knowing that life does happen, and though it may appear that it doesn't work out, all things do work together for good.

A BRIEF HISTORY

On December 31, 1997, my father, Pastor Donald R. Baker, transitioned home to be with the Lord due to a massive heart attack; it was a tragic loss. He was only 49 years old. My days became long and lonely without him in my life. I became depressed with suicidal thoughts, with a loss of appetite, I withdrew from family and friends. There were days I could not fulfill daily tasks such as work, taking care of my son, or much of anything. I was in a very dark place in my life. I saw no hope. I lost all my energy and the will to live. My mother and sister were overly concerned about my behavior, and so my Spiritual father, Dr. Darnell Leach. He arranged for my time away from home to *get myself together*. I went to the Psychiatric Institute of Washington, where they took good care of me. It was there I was diagnosed with Schizophrenia Disorder in March 1998. I received treatment, was placed on medication, and I entered into therapy. Feeling better, I returned home.

Another devastation, in March 1999, my mother, Pastor Janis M. Baker, transitioned while on the dialysis machine, she too was 49 years old. This was another interruption in my life. Again I returned to PIW and was off work for three months with a diagnosis of Bipolar Disorder. I was placed on different medications and therapy. My grandmother Evangelist Grace Johnson passed away on April 29, 2001. I gave birth to my second son August 16, 2001. I've tried a lot of different medications over the years with many hospitalizations. I've even tried slitting my wrists unsuccessfully and taking pills. My mother always told me if I committed suicide, I was going to hell because God said, "*Thou shall not kill.*" Exodus 20:13.

Recovery stories can be a messy thing. It has dozens of beginnings and with no final endings. Most of the conflict and drama is internal, and there's a lot more inaction than action. The lead character hides in the shadows much of the time, so you can't even see what's going on.

When my life joined up with depression, there were snapshots of me in clothes that I liked to wear. My mom made sure we have dressed appropriately, now that I remember.

No one ever mentioned strange emotional problems or mental illness back in the day. No one was worried then because I was self-contained at hiding my pain. Then migraine headaches started up with intense anxiety about school. I missed so many days and felt shame as if I were faking. I began to obsess over every one of my failings. I spent long hours alone in my room.

Throughout my teenage years, depression went under the radar. Feelings were dangerous. There were too many angry ones shaking in my core. I kept my emotion under wraps, even more so than in childhood. Nothing phased me outside the house, and even at home, I showed almost no sign of reaction to anything, also while churning with fear and anguish.

It was in my 20s that I broke open, and the streams of depression, fear, panic, obsessive Love, and anger flowed out. In response to a panic attack that lasted for a week, I saw a psychiatrist. In one marathon session, he helped me put the panic together with frightening episodes from my family life. I was not cured on the spot but never went back to him. It was too soon to do any more.

But no one mentioned depression. I first saw the Word applied to my condition in a letter one psychiatrist wrote in a reference letter. But I wasn't treated for that problem. In those days, therapy was still in the Freudian tradition, and it was all about family life and conflict. Depression was a springboard for going deeper. Digging up the past to understand my present problems was a tremendous help, and it changed me in many ways. But depression was still there in various forms, reappearing regularly for the next couple of decades. There were wonderfully happy and prosperous times as well, but I had these ups and downs.

Gradually, depression became so disruptive that my life couldn't take it anymore, I needed help. So, I finally did. This was the 1990s. I started a tour of medication over the next dozen years that didn't do much at all. Nor did therapy, psychiatrists, helped me to understand the more destructive patterns in my way of living.

Depression pushed into every corner of my existence, and both work and family life became more and more difficult. The medications only seemed to deaden the feelings that made me feel detached from everyone and immune to every pressure. It was like having pain signals turned off. There was no longer any sign coming from my body or brain that something might be wrong. I felt "fine," but relationships and work suffered.

The strange thing was that after all these years of living with depression. I thought it was entirely a problem of a loss of energy and motivation. As things got worse, I could, at last, imagine the possibility of getting better. I could see that I wasn't worthless by nature, that there were reasons my mind had trouble focusing, and that the frequent slowdown in my speech and thinking was also rooted in this illness. Perhaps the right treatment could bring about fundamental changes after all.

There were still traps ahead, though. I began to look more at depression than the details of my version of the illness. I thought depression was announcing my fate.

Faith changes everything, my whole outlook on life has changed down to the details

I had a "real" issue, and I had a reason to fight my internalized stigma, the lingering doubt that anything was wrong with me. I used to think that maybe I was using the illness to avoid life and cover up my weakness. Here was proof that depression wasn't all in my imagination but in my brain chemistry.

My faith In God restored a deep sense of worth

I got desperate and turned to my faith in God to help me. I needed Him to take the lead in my recovery. My faith gave me the energy and presence of mind to work on the emotions and relationships that impact my life I had some control over. If we believe WE can do it, we must have faith. Romans 10:17,

...Faith comes by hearing, hearing the Word.

PRAYER:

Father, I pray that the words You have given me write are clear to the readers. I pray that anyone who wants to put their faith in You would understand the way to do that is to trust that Your Word is true. I pray You would work in hearts that want to know You and that You would draw others to Yourself. Help us know how to trust You in troUbled times, good times, and I can't see my way-out times. Thank you for the GIFT of life and those who surround and support me. In Jesus' precious name, I pray, Amen.

One of the most important efforts for me was writing poems about my experience with *Depression* and *Suicide*. Writing is one way I discovered things. Deep fear had blocked me from doing it for years. I can see now that the real reason I got stuck was that I had been trying to write about everything but Depression and Suicide. When I could finally take that it on directly, writing, and expressing myself through poems came naturally.

After all this, recovery started to happen; something had changed deep down. I believed in myself again, and the inner conviction of worthlessness disappeared.

I am determined to stop wasting my life in depression. Despite the setbacks, I keep trying,

I found a satisfying purpose in writing poems, as well as the energy and humor to do what I wanted to do. I regained the awareness and emotional presence to be a part of my family again, instead of hiding out.

Anyone dealing with *Depression* and *Suicide,* setbacks happen. Sometimes there are just no simple answers. Know that there is *hope* and *help* available. I am no longer a victim because I live in my victory every day through the reading of the Bible and turning to God in my faith. This Scripture has helped me many times, Isiah 26:3,

> *3 Thou wilt keep him in perfect peace, whose mind is stayed on thee: because he trusteth in thee.*

Even though you may have or know someone with a *Mental Illness,* remember that you are human and you are essential. If you have a concern that someone may be suffering from depression, suicidal thoughts, etc., *speak up* and let someone know.

"Psalm 46 says, *God is our refuge and strength, a very present help in trouble. The reality is that there will be* difficult times, but God promises to be our refuge. Lay it all on Him.

Now to the poems...

Growing Pains

Sometimes I can't get over these growing pains; like my knees ache, my headaches, my back hurts, all I do is complain, when there are people worse off than I am.

I need to be grateful and appreciative for everything I have.

Give God praise and adoration He heals all pains, and he said by His stripes we are healed.

Trusting God

Lord light the way in which I take, knowing you are no mistake

Take my hand, and lead me on, carry me as my feet are worn.

Lift my head to see only you Lord, beyond the night sky or the Sun by day.

In your arms, I find safety and peace of mind.

Lord, you are my light, and you shine.

The Pandemic

We can't gather in large groups anymore. The rich and the
poor.

The Powers that be are slowly killing us you see. The virus
is here a pandemic it's called, my nerves are flames,

Anxiety; fear, depression is in us all, but God said He
would not let us fall.

Praise Over Problems

I will yet praise You over all my circumstances.

I will praise You with all of my heart.

You are the light that I can see;

Oh lord, come see about me. In the midnight hour, You are there.

In the afternoon You are there. Thank You, Lord, You are everywhere.

There is no place I can hide You to see all things,
I praise You with all my might, to stand firm in Your sight.

Spring

I'm feeling something new; I'm feeling something deep. Yet it's pure joy and delight. Oh no I'm awake now not asleep.

Skipping through the daisy's cherry blossoms bloom, nothing but Love fills this room.

Sharing cheers of laughter for hours on end

I had a broken heart that You were sent to mend.

Word Up

Tell me the truth, do you love me or not, feeling your heartbeat next to mine as we lay here and shine.

Looking for you all over the place, all I see is your face.

Planning and loving you day by day word up, what do you say?

You love me and me only, I'm proud of yours, and you are mine. This Love is true and kind.

Drunk In Love

You keep telling me I'm the one when I look at you, I see the sun.

Beneath my feet, I'm drunk in over you. Your love desires ringing in my ear, have no fear

Doubt and unbelief. I'm drunk in Love over what is mine. You who me over and over again?

I'm running out of time; drunk in Love you are mine. Oh, taste my wine for sure I'll make you want more.

Battle of The Mind

My mind is all over the place when it's filled with negatives in my face. I keep fighting battles with people all the time.

Listen, I need me a glass of wine; hopefully, that will help me get me through the day. Oh my what do I say?

I don't need weed in my life. I'm struggling with strife; hatred all around.

If I could just get out of town.

Feelings

My emotions are caught in the clouds, and I look upon my feelings. I feel lonely, angry, frustrated. My head is twisted.

Make me see the error of my ways, the longer the days, I melt for attention from anyone. I'm stuck here on earth with all these feelings and emotions. I need to gain control of my actions. These are the facts.

I have a hard time loving me, do you see what I see? Alone afraid to live every day. I need God to take my hand and lead the way. I need Him to boost up my confidence, staying alive and well, not going to hell.

I love God, and He loves me. Do you see what I see?

Journey

As I sit here, I'm thinking too hard wondering why I am here, what am I here for?

It's been a long journey, and I have a way to go. Does anyone know the troubles I've been through?

Seeking God's face as I run this race. Seeing further down the road I see in faith, waiting patiently for God to rescue me from this place, I rush what He is trying to do in me, take away the pain God.

My future rests in Your hands, not man's. I belong here until You come back for me or when my number is called. The question is, will I be ready to depart this earth.

I'm getting my life right now. I want to receive a crown. I want God to say well done my servant with not a frown.

Where I find Rest

Where do I find help for I am torn apart from a broken heart?

Who is the one who mends pieces back together and makes me whole?

It is He who holds the key to my soul. It's in Him that I find rest to take another day's test.

Yes, adversity is all around, where can I run and hide from my guilt and shame, nowhere because He knows my name.

I stand even though I'm weak, and it is for Him that I speak yet so humble and meek.

I stand and take hits and punches from the enemy, oh yes I fight back for he doesn't win, it was Jesus who bore my sin.

For I am content in all things for this life is temporal.

For I get distracted from time to time, I fix my eyes on Christ which is eternal life

Access into the kingdom, worshipping at His throne, for I know that He is with me, and I'm never alone.

He walks beside me in every way I give Him glory for as long as I live every day.

Worship the King, bowing at His feet He supplies all of my needs, everyone I meet I'm wrapped in the safety of His arms and safely I am kept.

Who Am I?

I am the one who bore your children, the one who prepares your meals even though you are hell on wheels.

I am the servant who caters to your needs as you plant your seeds.

I am Mother Earth, the flavor of salt, and a little sugar from bitter to sweet, and I'm just waiting on you to rub my feet.

I am the candle that burns the midnight oil sitting up thinking what's next to plant in the soil.

Always thinking and moving ahead. So I say to you, I'm living not dead.

I am the moneymaker, not a faker. The Proverbs 31 Phenomenal Woman that's who I am!

To know me is to love me, I'm an asset not a liability to be
with me is longevity

I am the one who bakes your bread and makes your bed.
I am a flower; butterfly always growing and flying.

Soar like an Eagle; Wise as a serpent, Quiet as a Dove
I am full of Love.

A Man A Good Tall Glass of Water

Never met anyone quite like you before.

You are a tall glass of water I sure would like to drink
Oh yes, I must think/

You make the hairs on the back of my neck stand up
straight/

No need to rush a kiss I will wait.

We speak no words, we don't even touch/

Our minds meet, our hearts beat as one.

Mass Destruction

Dropping bombs, spraying chemicals in the sky make me feel high.

Killing through the food and water supply.

They are telling us we must die all kinds of diseases, infections, bacteria alike.

Racial tension everywhere I look, and people don't believe we are living in the last book.

Lethal Injections

Yes, I did wrong eating and drinking what's bad for me injected with chemicals that I can't see, doing drugs to get that high, Man I thought I was floating in the sky.

I'm injected with fear; pain, oppression, right now begins this session. Sitting back watching the Pharmacist get paid while I'm snorting, and inhaling crack cocaine, let's not forget all the other drugs I haven't named.

The goal is to get to my heart so it will stop beating the part. Quietly as I take it all in, they need to reach my next of kin.

I'm drifting slowly for one last time because they don't want to remember my kind.

Because of the Melanin that's in my skin, they just want to kill life from within.

I've searched my soul so that I am right as I faced this one last night.

For all my life I've been injected with lies I can hear my ancestors' cries.

Your lies deception, tricks, plots, plans, and schemes, all are going to backfire in your face.

Only because you want to erase my Race and take my place.

A Letter To My Deceased Father

You use to take me to the playground and push me in the swing

You could hold a note, I mean really sing.

Whenever I had a problem, I could always talk to you
You know just what to say and even what to do.

Though my heart is still heavy and I still cry sometimes, it's hard to find

A Man to duplicate your kind.

They don't make them anymore the one who treats you well and opens up doors.

I've had Jokers; Tricksters who play mind games. What these Men don't know

I have and can do the same. The Sad part is I don't even remember their names.

Daddy, I'm tired of being on the clearance rack, all they want to do is shack, making

Empty promises that they fail to keep, now I'm hurt and all alone again crying myself to sleep.

Momma said there would be days like this. I wished I would have listened to you both.

Hate to admit but you were right, they only want the Goods and then they are out of Site

Why buy the milk when it's free. No Commitment; No Ring, No House, No Car, just No Responsibility

I know a person will only do what you continue to allow them to.

Now I'm taking back my life to wait and to be a Wife. A Lady is how you taught me to be no more discounts no more for free.

Daddy I'm all grown up as you can see, always looking deep at me.

I know I'm something special because God makes no junk. My eyes are open no longer smoking crunk.

Now that my spirit has awakened to a new day. I now must do everything God's way.

Thank you for teaching me the way to go. I still miss you more than you will ever know.

Love RO

Our greatest pain can be our most significant victory, but often we don't see it until we are out. I say without a doubt,

Suicide Is Not An Option!

Help is available 1-800-273-8255- Speak with a counselor today

National Suicide Prevention Lifeline - Hours: Available 24 hours. Languages: English, Spanish.

Made in the USA
Columbia, SC
06 April 2021